THE TOP TEN

INVENTIONS

THAT CHANGED THE WORLD

Chris Oxlade

W
FRANKLIN WATTS

This edition published in the UK in 2011 by Franklin Watts

Franklin Watts
338 Euston Road
London NW1 3BH

Franklin Watts Australia
Level 17/207 Kent Street
Sydney, NSW 2000

Dewey classification: 303.4'83

A CIP catalogue record for this book is available from the British Library.

ISBN: 978 1 4451 0642 7

Franklin Watts is a division of Hachette Children's Books, an Hachette UK company.
www.hachette.co.uk

THE TOP TEN INVENTIONS THAT CHANGED THE WORLD
was produced for Franklin Watts by
David West Children's Books, 7 Princeton Court, 55 Felsham Road, London SW15 1AZ

Designer: Gary Jeffrey
Illustrator: Rob Shone
Editor: Katharine Pethick

Photographic credits:
6l, Daniel Ullrich; 7t, Mark Pellegrini; 7m, eschipul: 7bl, gadl; 7br, Rama; 9t, Library of Congress;
bl, N. Kent Loudon; br, Dave-F; 15m, Library of Congress; br, Rgoogin; bl, Corbis; 18l, 19t, Library
of Congress; 19m, US Navy; 19b, NASA; 11l, John Kratz; 11bl, pinkiwinkitinki; 20, edkohler; 24,
Incase Designs

Printed in China

Contents

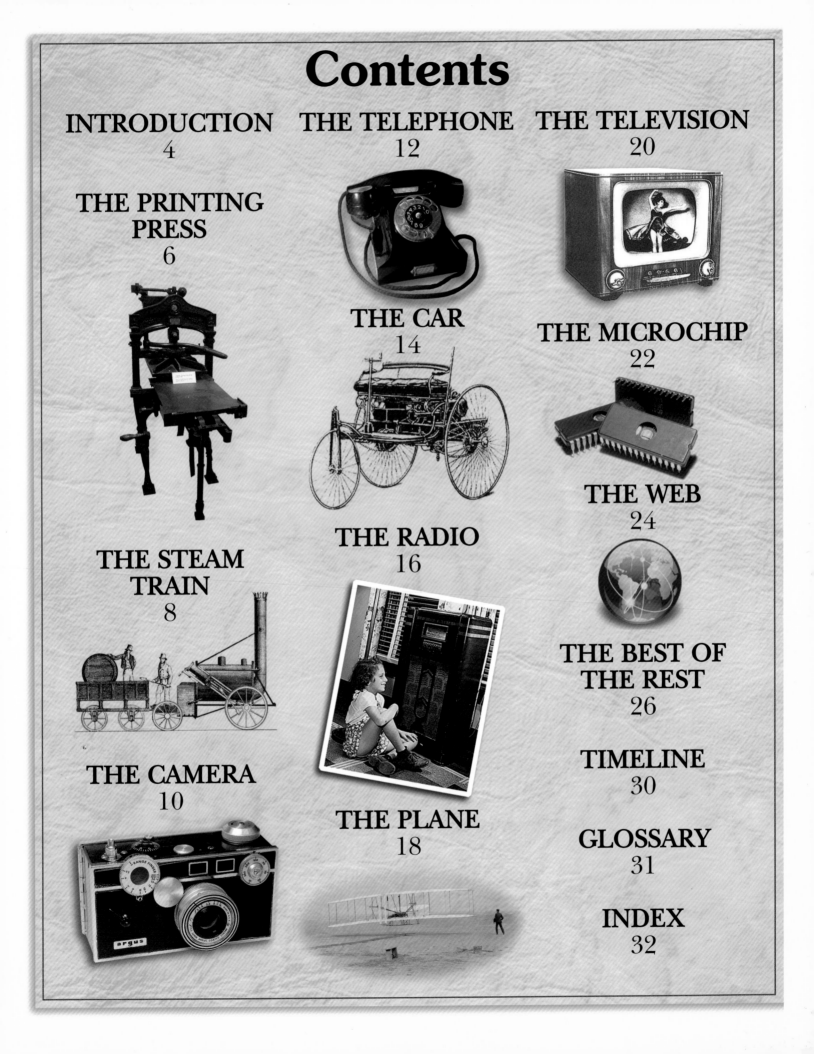

Introduction

The following inventions have been selected as the Top Ten from thousands of inventions that have undoubtedly changed our world. It is a difficult choice to make when there are so many options to consider. So why have these ten made it and not the others?

The hour glass helped medieval sailors to navigate the oceans but it was replaced by the chronometer.

* Firstly, the invention must have had an impact on the world within 50 years of being invented and yet must still affect our lives today.

* Secondly, it must be an invention, not a discovery (such as X-rays).

X-rays, discovered in 1895, gave rise to X-ray machines but were not an invention.

✱ Thirdly, it must be attributable to an inventor. The wheel does not make it into the Top Ten because no one knows who invented it.

You might disagree with the choice of inventions here. In which case you could make a list of your own favourites.

The wheel – a hugely important invention, that has no known inventor.

Hero of Alexandria invented a steam engine in the first century AD. Unfortunately, he did not know what to do with it and it took another 16 centuries before usable steam engines were invented.

The Printing Press

In 1450 Johannes Gutenberg built his first printing press in Mainz, Germany. The printing press was not a new idea, but Gutenberg had invented a way of making large quantities of metal type (individual metal letters). The type was arranged to make up the words, sentences and paragraphs on a page. Then it was placed in the press, inked and pressed on to paper. When enough copies had been printed, the type was used again to build another page. Before this, every book was copied out by hand. Now books could be printed in large numbers.

A piece of metal type has a reversed letter on its top.

6

THE PRINTED WORD

A copy of the Gutenberg Bible.

In 1452 Gutenberg began work on his most famous work, the first printed copy of the Bible. It was finally published in 1455. He produced 180 copies costing 30 florins each – equal to three years' wages for a clerk. But a hand-written book would have cost ten times as much. Others soon copied Gutenberg's methods, set up their own presses and began producing books. By 1500 there were more than 200 printing works in Europe, which between them had produced tens of thousands of books on a wide variety of subjects. This led to a rapid spread of new ideas and knowledge that could never have happened without the printing press. **Without this ability to spread information far and wide, our world might still be stuck in the dark ages.**

A single page of a Gutenberg Bible was made up of about 2,600 metal letters called type. The lines of text were placed in a metal frame, positioned on the press and inked. The page was printed on damp paper which was hung up to dry.

A modern printing press prints up to 10,000 sheets of paper an hour.

Today many thousands of new books are printed every week.

An electronic book (e-book) reader displays books stored in digital form.

The Steam Train

George Stephenson (1781–1848) is thought by many to be the father of the railways.

In 1821, wealthy merchant Edward Pease met engineer George Stephenson. Pease wanted a horse-drawn tramway to carry coal to the town of Stockton-on-Tees in northern England. He offered Stephenson the job of building the tramway, but Stephenson persuaded Pease to use steam locomotives instead of horses. Four years later, on 27 September 1825, the Stockton and Darlington Railway was officially opened.

At 10:00 am Locomotion No 1, driven by Stephenson, set off from Shildon near Darlington. It was pulling 34 wagons filled with coal, flour and more than 500 people, some on top of the goods, some in passenger wagons and the VIPs in a coach. At 3:45 pm the train arrived at Stockton. It had travelled 40 kilometres and managed a top speed of 24 kilometres per hour.

The Skerne Bridge (right) was one of the first railway bridges ever built. It is still in use today.

FULL STEAM AHEAD

The potential of steam power was first demonstrated in 1804, when a locomotive built by Englishman Richard Trevithick pulled wagons at an ironworks in

In the nineteenth century the train station became an important part of most towns

Wales. Early steam locomotives were slow, unreliable and often broke the iron rails they ran on. But the pioneering railway engineers, such as Stephenson, gradually improved the technology, and the success of the Stockton and Darlington Railway showed that steam locomotion was the way forwards. This was the time of the Industrial Revolution in Britain, the USA and other countries. The railways moved huge amounts of raw materials and finished goods quickly. **The steam train enabled the rapid industrial growth of the 19th century – a revolution that changed the world forever.**

In 1869 the Transcontinental Railway was completed. It connected the east and west coasts of the United States.

In developed countries industries relied heavily on steam trains until the 1960s.

The Camera

Frenchman Joseph Nicéphore Niépce was frustrated. He simply could not hold his hand steady enough to trace the image of his garden produced on his camera obscura. Niépce began searching for a way to record the image instead. Around 1816 he began to experiment with silver chloride, which darkens when exposed to light. He produced some images on paper but they quickly faded away. In 1824 Niépce tried using bitumen (black sticky, tar-like material), which he knew turns slowly lighter when exposed to light. In 1826 he placed a pewter sheet coated with bitumen dissolved in lavender oil inside his camera obscura, pointed it out into a courtyard and waited for eight hours. Then he rinsed away the excess bitumen to preserve the image. The result was a photograph that still exists today.

The camera obscura was a popular drawing aid in the 18th century.

FROM SNAPSHOTS TO CINEMA

In 1829 Niépce joined forces with another Frenchman, Louis Jacques Daguerre, and continued to experiment. In 1837, four years after Niépce died, Daguerre perfected his 'daguerreotype' photographic process, using silver iodide coated on metal sheets. A new process using negative images recorded on glass plates came into use 20 years later. Heavy equipment and hazardous chemicals meant photography was only for the experts. But in 1889 American George Eastman began selling a lightweight camera containing a roll of celluloid film.

A young Abraham Lincoln captured by daguerreotype in 1846

The Eastman Kodak Brownie of 1900 was light, simple to use and cost $1.

The same film was used in the first movie cameras, which took images in quick succession along the roll. This was a giant step on the road to the modern movie business, making the camera one of the most important inventions that has opened up the world to us all.

CINÉMATOGRAPHE LUMIÈRE

In 1895 the French Lumière brothers were the first to show movies to a paying audience.

Modern camcorders and cameras record images digitally.

The Telephone

Early telephones had separate earpieces and mouthpieces.

'Come here, I want to see you!' called Alexander Graham Bell. Ordinary words, but extraordinary because they were the first ever to be uttered over the telephone. It was 10 March 1876. Bell was in his workshop in Boston, Massachusetts and spoke to his assistant Thomas Watson. Bell had been trying to find a way of sending several telegraph messages along the same wire at the same time when the idea of sending speech along a wire came to him. He developed transmitters to change sound into an electrical signal and a receiver to turn the signal back into sound. Bell filed a patent for his telephone just a few hours before rival inventor Elisha Gray.

IT'S GOOD TO TALK

Until the invention of the telephone, the only way to get a message to somebody far away quickly was the telegraph.

A telegraph key used to tap out Morse code

The sender had to visit a telegraph office to send the message and at the other end the message had to be delivered. The new telephone was useless, though, without networks to link receivers together, but these quickly

grew, locally at first and then nationally and eventually internationally. Less than ten years after that famous first call, there were 150,000 telephone subscribers in the USA alone. As early as the 1890s automatic exchanges

An Edwardian telephone exchange

opened, allowing people to dial each other without talking to a human operator. Bell's invention started the technology that allows us to talk and text instantly to people anywhere in the world, **a mass communication system that**

A 1930s dial telephone

Mobile phones such as the iPhone also act as music players, cameras and games machines.

has dramatically changed the way we live.

13

The Car

Henry Ford did not invent the motor car. That honour went to German engineer Karl Benz, who built the first proper car in 1886. But Ford made the car popular by building cars for ordinary people. Ford's success came from just one car – the Model T – which was unveiled at the Ford Motor Company's Detroit factory on 1 October 1908. It was different from other cars of the time in that it was basic and easy to drive, yet also easy to maintain and repair because of interchangeable parts. It was also a lot cheaper because over the next few years Ford developed

Henry Ford (1863-1947) was the founder of the Ford Motor Company. He built his first car, the Quadricycle, in 1896.

MOVING THE MASSES

At first, Ford's Model Ts were built one by one by hand, in the same way as other cars. This method was slow and made cars expensive – only the rich could afford the luxury of driving. In 1908, even Ford's workers made just eleven cars in a month.

Karl Benz's Motorwagen was a horse-drawn carriage with a petrol engine.

mass production. The Model T was pieced together on an assembly line (as most modern cars are). A worker added one or two parts as a car passed by on a conveyor belt. It was an efficient system that kept costs low and production high.

Robots do many of the jobs on modern car production lines.

In 1900 fewer than 1,000 cars were made in the USA. In 1940 that figure had risen to 4.5 million.

But in 1914, the year Ford's assembly line moved into full swing, a Model T rolled on to the road every three minutes. That year, Ford built more cars than all the other US car manufacturers combined. As efficiency improved, the Model T became cheaper and the cars were snapped up by a public eager to have their own transport. By 1925 half the cars in the world were Model Ts. When production stopped in 1927 more than 15 million had been built. By then car technology had moved on and it has continued to move on ever since. **Today the car is vital for the global economy.**

Too many cars cause congestion and pollution.

15

The Radio

Heinrich Hertz, the German scientist who discovered radio waves in 1888, described them as 'mysterious electromagnetic waves that we cannot see with the naked eye'. But he didn't see any application for radio, commenting, 'It's of no use whatsoever.' Guglielmo Marconi thought differently. He was one of several inventors who realised radio waves could be used for communication. In 1895, aged just 21, he was in his family's garden in Italy testing his latest radio transmitter and receiver. Both featured long, vertical aerials. Marconi tapped the transmitter key and looked across the garden to where his brother manned the receiver.

Marconi's brother immediately waved a handkerchief – the receiver had detected the radio signal. The following week Marconi sent his brother to a hill a mile away. This time his brother fired a gun to signal that the radio waves had been detected. The age of radio communications had arrived.

WIRELESS PROGRESS

At first radio was used to send electric telegraph signals. This was called wireless telegraphy. One of its first applications was ship-to-shore communications. Soon after the Titanic disaster, every large ship was required by law to have a wireless operator listening for Morse code messages 24 hours a day. By 1906, amplitude modulation had been invented, which allowed sound to be sent by radio. The first radio stations went on air in 1919, and by the end of the 1920s radio broadcasting was widespread. At the same time radio waves were used for the first television broadcasts. Today, radio has a bewildering range of applications. Our 'wireless' world boasts baby monitors, global positioning satellites (GPS), mobile phones and wi-fi computer networks, **making radio one of the most useful inventions the world has so far seen.**

The sinking Titanic used Marconi equipment to send one of the first wireless distress signals.

This is America..

...where you can listen to your radio in your living room – – not in a hideout. Where you are free to hear both sides of a question and form your own opinion ★ This is your America

... Keep it Free!

A World War II propaganda poster. In wartime the radio was a vital way to keep civilians informed.

The 1954 Regency TR-1 was the world's first pocket radio.

This 15 metre radar dish is used by NASA to track spacecraft.

17

The Plane

The American brothers

Wilbur and Orville Wright had spent four years experimenting

with kites and gliders before preparing for a powered flight.

Now their aircraft, Flyer, was ready. The date was 17 December

1903 and the place was Kitty Hawk in North Carolina. At

10.35 am Orville released the holding wire and Flyer sped

along its wooden guide rail. After a few seconds Flyer rose into the

air. Twelve seconds and 36 metres later it landed again. Orville Wright

had become the first person to achieve controlled and powered heavier-

than-air flight. The brothers continued with more flights, the second of

50 metres and the next covering 60 metres.

PLANE POWER

In the years after the Wright brothers' famous flight, other pioneers built and flew their own aircraft. But ten years later aircraft were still oddities. The outbreak of the First World War in 1914 changed that. Armies quickly realised that the aeroplane would be a useful tool for spying on and attacking the enemy. Aircraft technology quickly improved as each side tried to build better aircraft than the other. After the war bombers were converted into the first airliners and the first airlines began operating. For those who could afford to pay, journey times were reduced from days to hours. In the 1930s, flying boats carried passengers right across the globe. The speed and size of aircraft increased quickly again during the Second World War (1939-45). The war saw the invention of the jet engine, which powers today's sophisticated airliners. **From a short hop just over 100 years ago to worldwide air travel for everyone today, flight has transformed the world.**

Otto Lilienthal (1848–1896) was one of the first aviation pioneers. He flew in home-made gliders.

A First World War recruitment poster.

Flying boats such as this Catalina were used by air forces, navies and airlines.

At around noon Wilbur began a fourth flight. He covered 260 metres in 59 seconds. Later, a strong gust of wind picked up the plane and rolled it over and over, smashing it beyond repair.

Is this the future shape of planes? Aircraft with a 'blended wing body' could be more efficient that current models.

The Television

Television requires a device that detects the amount of light coming from each part of a scene. This information is sent by electricity to another device that displays the image. This process is repeated many times a second to make the image move. Scottish inventor John Logie Baird gave the first demonstration of television in 1926. To the amazement of the invited audience, a flickering, blurred picture of his assistant's face was transmitted to the next room. His 'televisor' included large spinning discs full of holes to scan the scene and rebuild the picture.

A modern high-definition flat-screen television

EVOLUTION OF THE GOGGLE BOX

Baird's first system produced poor quality images made up of just 30 vertical lines, with twelve pictures a second, but later he built an improved 240-line system.

Television viewing in 1928

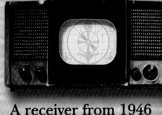

A receiver from 1946

At the same time as Baird was developing his television system with its mechanical discs, other pioneers were working on completely different electronic systems. These used a device called the cathode ray tube to capture and display moving images. American inventor Philo T. Farnsworth is generally credited with the first demonstration of an electronic television system in 1927. Early television broadcasts, which began in 1928 in some countries, were transmitted by both mechanical and electronic systems. But by the mid 1930s the superior picture quality of electronic systems killed off mechanical systems such as Baird's. The new gadget proved incredibly popular as prices fell during the 1950s. In the early 1960s, television overtook cinema as the world's most popular form of mass entertainment, and ever since **the world has remained hooked on the most** popular device ever invented.

An early TV remote

Colour television arrived in the 1950s.

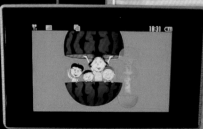

New from Japan – the TV that thinks it's a phone

21

The Microchip

In 1958 the development of electronics had reached a stumbling block. Electrical engineers could build complicated circuits from transistors and other components. But wiring thousands of components together was a headache, as a single broken connection prevented the circuit from working. And although each component was small, the circuits were large. Computers of the time filled whole rooms. Then Jack Kilby, a new employee at Texas Instruments, had a brainwave – make all the components from the same material and manufacture them together instead of separately and then connect them with wires. He got to work and a few months later demonstrated the first microchip (or integrated circuit) to his bosses. It was built on a slice of germanium, a type of semiconductor.

Invented in 1947, transistors were a great advance, but they still took up lots of space.

The invention of the microchip was a huge leap forward that made miniaturisation of electronic circuits possible. Jack Kilby went on to co-invent the personal calculator – the first consumer product to popularise the new technology.

SMALLER, FASTER, CHEAPER

Kilby was not the only scientist working on integrated circuits. Six months after his demonstration, Robert Noyce, working at Fairchild Semiconductor, built a microchip from silicon. This was the ancestor of all modern microchips. Microchips were first used by the military, but within a few years appeared in consumer devices such as televisions and radios, making these cheaper, smaller and more reliable. Today there are microchips in almost every electronic device, from car keys to supercomputers. Our modern lifestyles, with mobile phones, the Internet and games consoles, would be impossible without them. The global digital revolution created by the microchip is here to stay.

Modern day chips are amazingly complex and increasingly tiny.

Microchips made possible the US space programme of the 1960s.

The development of the microprocessor (a mini computer on a chip) enabled the home computer revolution of the 1980s.

Microchips have made machines from spacecraft to electric toothbrushes more efficient, more reliable and safer.

23

The Web

In 1980, English software consultant Tim Berners-Lee was working at CERN, the European Particle Physics Laboratory in Switzerland. While there he wrote a program for storing and linking files together on his computer. He called it

Web pages offer a mass of information instantly, at the press of a mouse button.

'Enquire' after a Victorian encyclopedia he read as a child. In 1989 Berners-Lee took the idea of 'Enquire' and extended it to link the files on one computer to files on any other computer on a network. He wrote a coding system called HTML which let people put links in their files, created software for accessing the files across the internet, as well as a program called a browser to display the HTML files. This collection of linked information was dubbed the World Wide Web. It was launched in 1991.

User created web services like Wikipedia maintain the spirit of Berners-Lee's original vision for the World Wide Web.

GETTING CONNECTED

The World Wide Web could not work without the Internet. The history of the Internet dates back to 1969, when the US Government's Advanced Research Projects Agency (ARPA) linked two computers at different research laboratories in California so that they could share information. Other computers were quickly added, forming a network called ARPANET. The Internet was born in the mid 1970s when various other networks around the world were linked to ARPANET. It allowed computer users around the world to share information and send e-mails. Since Berners-Lee invented the Web, Internet use has ballooned. In 2008 there were more than a trillion web pages, including on-line encyclopedias, shops, instant news and social networking. **The Web has revolutionised the way information is shared, making the world a smaller place than ever.**

The original computer mouse from 1967. Its inventor, Doug Engelbart, was also the first person to connect to ARPANET.

The Web is run by 'server farms' – banks of computers that store and distribute the information on the Web.

Wireless networking allows connection to the Web from almost anywhere.

The Best of the Rest

THE ELECTRIC MOTOR AND DYNAMO

The first electric motor was demonstrated by the British scientist Michael Faraday in 1821. He showed that electric current flowing through a magnetic field produces movement. A decade later Faraday showed the reverse effect – that moving a magnet inside a coil of wire produces electricity in the wire. In 1832 France's Hippolyte Pixii put Faraday's findings to practical use by building the first electricity generator. Today, most of the electricity we use is produced in power stations by generators and electric motors drive machines from power drills and tumble driers to robots and hard drives.

Faraday at work in his laboratory.

THE WHEEL

Wheels are not just for vehicles – nearly every modern machine uses wheels or cogs in some way. Even computers use wheels inside their hard drives and DVD drives.

The wheel is one of the most important inventions of all time. We don't know exactly how or when the wheel was invented, but ancient engravings from Mesopotamia (part of modern-day Iraq), dating back to 3500 BC, show that the potter's wheel and simple wheeled carts were already in use.

THE BOAT

The first boat was probably simply a hollowed-out tree trunk or a raft of logs. We don't know when people started travelling on water, but it must have been tens of thousands of years ago. Whenever it happened, the boat allowed people to travel long distances to hunt, trade and find new homes.

Built of reeds, this is a replica of an early boat.

Today, giant metal ships carry vast amounts of raw materials, such as oil and grain, and finished goods, such as cars and toys, across the globe. The modern world economy would be impossible without them.

TIMEPIECES

Harrison's marine chronometer

In ancient times people tried many different ways of measuring the passing of time. Their inventions included water clocks, sundials, sand timers and burning candles. Mechanical clocks were hopelessly inaccurate until 1656 when Dutchman Christiaan Huygens invented the pendulum clock, whose speed was regulated by a swinging pendulum. One place where an accurate clock was vital was at sea, where knowing the exact time was necessary for calculating longitude. Navigation was improved dramatically when, in 1759, English clockmaker John Harrison built a marine chronometer that was accurate to 30 seconds in a year. Incredibly accurate electronic timing is the norm today.

Almost every electronic machine has a built-in clock, either for its own use or for our information.

GUNPOWDER AND GUNS

Gunpowder was invented in China around 950 AD, but it was another 300 years before the Chinese used it to fire their newly-invented cannons. Gradually the technology spread to the rest of the world. In the 16th century ships were armed with cannon and hand-held guns with triggers were being used in battle, although they were unreliable and slow to reload. By the 19th century the musket and field artillery gun were causing heavy casualties in war. At the battle of Waterloo in 1815, 45,000 men (one third of the combatants) were killed or wounded. Later in the century the machine gun was invented by American Richard Gatling. It was used to devastating effect during the First World War. Most famous of modern guns is the AK-47 assault rifle, designed by Mikhail Kalashnikov in 1947. It is the weapon of choice for revolutionaries, private armies and terrorists all over the world.

AK-47

MONEY

When people first traded, they bartered with each other – perhaps exchanging some milk for some eggs, or some crops for clothes. Eventually a commodity was used as money, to represent the value of things. This allowed buying and selling to take place. The Aztecs, for example, used cocoa beans and in Mesopotamia (in modern-day Iraq), around 3000 BC, a shekel was a measure of grain that was used as money. More recently, in Britain, a 'pound' was originally a pound in weight of silver. The first coins were pieces of gold or silver that had value. Banknotes were first used in China in the 7th century.

Lydian coins from 640 BC

PAPER

The earliest recorded forms of paper, made from the papyrus plant, were used in Egypt in around 3500 BC. True paper is believed to have originated in China in around the 2nd century AD, although there is evidence that it was used even before this date.

Chinese woodblock print in 1249, Song Dynasty

The use of paper spread from China through the Islamic world, and it was first produced in Europe in the early 12th century. In the early 19th century mechanised paper production meant information, such as letters, books and newspapers could be exchanged cheaply, affecting cultures worldwide.

Roman public toilets, Ostia Antica

TOILETS AND SEWERS

The first toilets were built around 2350 BC in a palace in Mesopotamia (in modern-day Iraq). Underneath the simple pedestal was a sewage pipe. The Ancient Egyptians and Romans also had toilets, but mainly for the privileged. The first flushing toilet was designed in 1596 by Englishman Sir John Harrington, but it was the 19th century before towns and cities had sewers and toilets became available for all. Even today, nearly 40 per cent of the world's population still does not have access to one.

Pont du Gard, Roman aqueduct

AQUEDUCTS

An aqueduct is a channel, often supported on piers, that carries water from one place to another. The Ancient Romans are famous for the aqueducts that carried water to drinking-water fountains in their cities, but the Ancient Egyptians and people of the Indus valley had built aqueducts for irrigating their crops thousands of years before.

MEDICAL SCANNERS

In the early 1900s, the Italian radiologist Alessandro Vallebona proposed using X-rays to produce an image of a slice through a person (rather than a simple X-ray). This is known as tomography. The first tomography machine was the PET scanner.

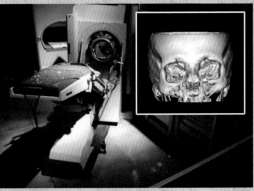
The first commercial CT head scanner, with scan of a skull, inset.

The PET (positron emission tomography) scanner of 1958, was used especially for taking images of the brain. This was followed by the CAT (computerised axial tomography) scanner and the MRI (magnetic resonance imaging) scanner.

The 'Glasses Apostle' by Conrad von Soest (1403)

LENSES

The earliest evidence of lenses comes from the Ancient Greek Aristophanes, who wrote about a 'burning-glass' (a convex lens used to focus the Sun's rays to produce fire). Early lenses were also used as magnifying glasses. Accurate lenses made telescopes and microscopes possible – inventions that led to many scientific discoveries. Most importantly, lenses correct sight defects.

REFRIGERATOR/FREEZER

Refrigerators and freezers allow the long-term storage of food both at home and in the food-supply chain. Domestic electric refrigerators became widely available in the 1920s. Before then, outdoor ice houses were used for cold storage.

An early refrigerator

Timeline of Inventions

		Invention	Influence
ANCIENT	4000 BC	SAILING BOAT Egypt	Makes trade possible by sea
		PAVED ROADS Ur, Middle East	Faster transport of people and goods
	3500 BC	PAPYRUS Egypt	Allows writing of records with ink
		THE WHEEL Mesopotamia	Heavy loads can be moved easily
	3000 BC	MONEY Mesopotamia	Allows buying and selling of goods
		AQUEDUCT Indus Valley and India	Irrigation of crops to increase yields
	620 BC	COINS Lydia	Helps trade – money can be counted
	450 BC	ABACUS Europe	One of the first calculating machines
MEDIEVAL	850 AD	CAMERA OBSCURA China	Allows accurate drawing of a scene
	950	GUNPOWDER China	Makes firearms possible
	1000	SPINNING WHEEL India	Important step in textile development
	1250	CANNON China	Harnesses the power of gunpowder
	1450	**THE PRINTING PRESS Johannes Gutenberg, Germany**	**Begins the rapid spread of information**
MODERN ERA	1596	FLUSH TOILET Sir John Harrington, UK	Reduces smells, but only for the rich!
	1608	TELESCOPE Hans Lippershey, Holland	Leads to the discovery of planets and moons
	1656	PENDULUM CLOCK Christiaan Huygens, Netherlands	Accurate timekeeping is here to stay
	1759	MARINE CHRONOMETER John Harrison, UK	Makes accurate navigation at sea possible
	1825	**THE STEAM TRAIN Gerge Stephenson**	**Steam locomotion demonstrated as transportation of the future**
	1826	**THE CAMERA Joseph Nicéphore Niépce, France**	**Events and views can be recorded in pictures**
	1876	**THE TELEPHONE Alexander Graham Bell, USA**	**Allows people to talk over long distances**
	1886	**THE CAR Karl Benz, Germany**	**The start of the automobile revolution**
	1895	**THE RADIO Guglielmo Marconi, Italy**	**Wireless signals sent over long distances**
20TH CENTURY–	1903	**THE PLANE The Wright Brothers, USA**	**Powered flight becomes a reality**
	1926	**THE TELEVISION John Logie Baird, UK**	**The birth of the television industry**
	1945	ATOMIC BOMB Manhattan Project team, USA	Power of atomic weapons is revealed
	1958	**THE MICROCHIP Jack Kilby, California, USA**	**Miniaturised electronic devices become possible**
	1975	**PERSONAL COMPUTER, Steve Wozniak, California, USA**	The computer that brings computing to the masses
	1977	MOBILE PHONE, Bell Labs, USA	Until now all phones were on fixed lines
	1980	COMPACT DISC Phillips Electronic and Sony Corp, Netherlands and Japan	The first digital music format
	1991	**THE WEB Tim Berners-Lee, Switzerland**	**The start of the Internet revolution**
	2001	iPod Apple Computer, USA	The personal digital music player takes off

Glossary

World Events

Development of first towns and cities
Human population reaches about 7 million
The Ancient Egyptian civilisation begins

World's population reaches 14 million

The Assyrians conquer Egypt
Height of the Greek civilisation

Growth of the Mayan Civilisation in South America
Viking Leif Ericsson sails to North America
Height of the Mongol Empire
The Hundred Years' War between France and England ends

William Shakespeare is writing plays
The world's population has grown to more than 500 million.
Europeans are settling in the Americas

Captain Cook discovers Australia

Industrial Revolution is at its height

Chocolate is invented!

Mark Twain writes Tom Sawyer

The Statue of Liberty is unveiled
The first modern Olympic games (1896)

End of Second World War
Rock and roll music shakes the west

Jaws is the first modern blockbuster movie

The first Star Wars movie goes on worldwide release

The 9/11 terrorist attack on The World Trade Center takes place

camera obscura a box with a hole or lens in one side that produces an image on the other side

electromagnetic waves a form of energy that travels in waves of electricity and magnetism

HTML short for hypertext mark-up language

network a collection of computers connected to each other to share information

patent an official licence which grants someone the sole right to make or sell an item they have invented

pendulum a rod or string with a weight at the bottom that swings from side to side

receiver a device that detects radio waves

semiconductor a material that can act as both an electrical conductor and insulator

signal an electric current or radio wave that changes strength or shape to represent information

telegraph a communications system called Morse Code that used simple on and off signals to represent letters and words

transistor an electronic device that works like a switch

transmitter a device that sends out radio waves

Index